MuShu

Constance L. Watkins

Illustrations by Constance Watkins and Arthur Henry

AuthorHouse™
1663 Liberty Drive
Bloomington, IN 47403
www.authorhouse.com
Phone: 1-800-839-8640

© 2013 Constance L. Watkins. All rights reserved.

No part of this book may be reproduced, stored in a retrieval system,
or transmitted by any means without the written permission of the author.

Published by AuthorHouse 7/16/2013

ISBN: 978-1-4817-7993-7 (sc)
ISBN: 978-1-4817-7994-4 (e)

Any people depicted in stock imagery provided by Thinkstock are models,
and such images are being used for illustrative purposes only.
Certain stock imagery © Thinkstock.

This book is printed on acid-free paper.

Because of the dynamic nature of the Internet, any web addresses or links contained in this book may have changed since publication and may no longer be valid. The views expressed in this work are solely those of the author and do not necessarily reflect the views of the publisher, and the publisher hereby disclaims any responsibility for them.

This book is dedicated to MuShu.
The furry ball of joy that brought so much love and happiness to Joey and his family.

Joey was very excited, he was about to get a very special pet. He was going to get his very own puppy. His family already had a dog, but this one was for Joey. He could hardly wait. The breed of his puppy was a mixture of Maltese and Yorkshire Terrier. It was called a "Morkie".

The evening before he was to pick up his new pet, Joey was getting more excited by the minute. His anticipation kept growing more and more. His mother told him he had to get to sleep because they would have a long drive tomorrow.

It would take about four hours to get where the puppy lived. She warned him they would have to wake up early and get on the road quickly. But she was sure that he would not sleep too much that night.

It was both a happy and a sad situation for the puppy. The people that had him could not keep him due to changes in their family.

BUT, Joey needed a good friend and he would give the puppy lots of love.

Before Joey went to bed, there was a phone call. Joey could tell by the expression on his mother's face that this was a sad call. He was very worried what was happening. When she finished the phone call, she looked very sad.

She had to tell Joey that the family had changed their mind. Now they did not want to part with the dog.

Joey was heart broken. He began to cry. He was so disappointed. Nothing his mother could do would console him.

Joey's mother felt bad. She called the lady back and explained how much the puppy meant to Joey.

She told her that he was crying and was very disappointed.

Later that night, the lady called back. She told them that she had reconsidered and decided that Joey could have the puppy. She said she could not disappoint him that way. Joey was going to get his puppy after all. He was so happy that he could not sleep.

The very next day, Joey and his mother got up very early. They started out quickly so they could pick up the puppy as soon as possible. Joey was so excited, he kept asking, "Are we there yet??" The trip seemed extra long because he was so excited.

Then, they finally arrived and Joey got to meet his new friend. They were both very excited. Everyone could see this would be a friendship that would last a lifetime. Joey's furry bundle of joy was smaller than he anticipated. But he could not have been happier.

He held the puppy in his arms all the way home. They hugged and the puppy kissed him a lot. They really belonged together. Joey already had a nice little house, and a snuggly warm bed waiting for his new friend. He also bought a pretty pink leash and collar.

Joey could not wait to tell Grammy the news. As soon as they could, they sent a message and a picture to Grammy on her cell phone. Now she could instantly see the new addition to the family. Grammy was sooo excited about the puppy! She asked Joey what he named his new friend. Joey replied with great excitement, "I will call her MuShu!" Grammy liked that name.

Joey could not wait for the next day to take MuShu for a walk. He had her pink leash, and she was wearing her pink collar.

Joey even brought plastic bags for clean up. He was fast becoming a real dog owner.

Joey happily shared the news with his good friend Matthew. He too was very excited and happy for Joey. Matthew also liked MuShu.

Another person Joey just had to tell about MuShu was his cousin Samantha. He could not wait to share his news with her. They were at the pool when he told her all about it. Samantha was very excited and happy for Joey. She cheered when she heard about his dog. And she liked the name he chose.

About the Author
(shown here with her grandchildren)

Constance Watkins is retired from the Unified Court System of New York State. She is a writer, and an artist, skilled in watercolor, pastel, acrylic, and photography. Her paintings and photographic work have won numerous awards. Connie's writings have been published in the Catholic Sun and Mohawk Valley Women, both popular in central New York. There have also been numerous items by and about her in local newspapers.

She is quite active in her church and local art associations. She has held positions there from secretary to contest judge. She has five grandchildren, who all know her as "Grammy." They greatly enjoy their visits to her upstate New York home where "the creek", is the main attraction.

As an instructor she has also conducted classes in children's crafts, writing, and pastel painting at several different organizations in her area. Constance says she likes to write from her heart. She prefers writing about events and joys that she has experienced personally.

CPSIA information can be obtained
at www.ICGtesting.com
Printed in the USA
BVIC00n0408201114
375785BV00004B/13